Rob Versus The Nincompoops

Sarcastically Knocking The Common Sense
Back Into The Daft, The Charlatans
& The Not So Know-It-Alls.

Rob Anspach

Rob Versus The Nincompoops
Sarcastically Knocking The Common Sense
Back Into The Daft, The Charlatans
& The Not So Know-It-Alls.

Copyright © 2023 Anspach Media
Cover design by: Freddy Solis

All rights reserved. No part of this book may be reproduced or transmitted in any form or by any means without written permission from the author.

ISBN 13: 979-8-9889988-1-5

Printed in USA

Disclaimer:
Oh yes, we must have a disclaimer…it makes the lawyers happy. The author has spent a lifetime using sarcasm as a means to grow his business. He shares interactions in this book that you may or may not agree with, his actions and communications are contrary to what most customer service gurus teach. But, it works for him and could work for you too, although highly doubtful.

What People Are Saying

"OMG....read that in a quick sitting. Still laughing! WTF really a Wisa card?!? Diagnosed with Sarcasm... Note from mom! I have taken the lead from my friend Rob and love to entertain myself with scammers now. It's a new sport to frustrate unknown callers and get blocked. I am reminded of a joke that has a play on words...What is the difference between a pun and a fart? A pun is a shift of wit!"
~ **Travis Rohrer**

"Now in his 8th installment in the series, Rob's books have become the reverse equivalent of an 'English as a Second Language' course. He has learned how to curse fluently in at least a dozen dialects. Rob's phone, tablet and car stereo are portals to the Bermuda Triangle of Wasted Time for scammers and nincompoops. Somewhere in a dark and dingy call-center there is a mug with Rob's face on it, ready to be awarded to the caller who can accurately recite his name, home address, date of birth and company which provides his internet service.~ **Steve Gamlin,** The Motivational Firewood ™ Guy

"Book 8 of the Rob Versus series is one of his best works yet. I have to say though that Rob is a very bad influence on me through his books as his snarkiness and sarcasm propagate its way into my own conversations with Scammers, and amateur sales people who call me up on a daily basis. Arm yourself with the rapier wit that Rob shares and drive these people crazy, waste their time, and keep them from ripping someone off a little longer." ~ **Paul Douglas**   Coauthor on *"Optimize This"*

"Our favorite superhero, Rob Anspach aka Scammer Bane, strikes again - armed with his razor-sharp wit and sarcastic comments, he is out there to fight the ignorance, arrogance and the outright ineptitude of the modern world. I loved the perfect mixture of humor, no-so-understated irony and sagacious warnings. Brilliantly sarcastic and unputdownable. This book will make you laugh out loud." ~ **J. H. Tepley**
Author of the *"Lightwatch Chronicles"* & other cool books

*"This could be Rob's best book yet! (And **this** is coming from a longtime fan!) It is past time for us to turn our own wit against the Nincompoops who are flooding our inboxes and ringing our phones. And, for the record, I agree with your assessment that WE are safer because YOU are wasting these nincompoops time!"* ~ **B. Michelle Pippin** www.bmichellepippin.com

"I love the book. No one will ever tire from Rob's wit, wisdom, and just a lot of sarcasm. So Many Nincompoops!" ~ **Barry Jacobson**, www.barryjacobsonconsulting.com

"Well, what can I say? Rob, you did it again! Rob Versus The Nincompoops will crack you up and keep you thinking to yourself, 'why didn't I think to reply like that?' Rob lays out story after story detailing his daily battles against scammers, Charlatans and Know-It-Alls. Rob uses his wry sarcastic humor to pointedly display his witty and rib-tickling methods to give it back to the scammers of the world and put them on their heels. I am always fascinated and amused by these exchanges and highly recommend reading this book, especially when I want to laugh out loud!" ~ **Ted Tedford,** Tedford & Associates   www.TedfordLaw.com Author of the "Empathetic Lawyer"

"Rob sucked me back in once again with his new book "Rob Versus The Nincompoops!" I thought I'd read just a chapter or two before I realized I was 35 pages in and it was 1:00 AM. Bigger, funnier and with double the sarcasm. Pick up a copy for your friends and family." ~ **Brad Szollose**, Host of Awakened Nation Podcast

"It's always fun to read Rob's "Versus" books and the "Nincompoops" edition you are holding is no exception. Some people think Rob is rude, but I actually admire him for taking the time to talk to these people when I don't have that kind of patience. If you too are like me and would rather not talk to the growing number of not so know-it-alls in the world, you can still get a good laugh just by reading Rob's conversations with these nincompoops. Thanks for bringing some humor to my day!" ~ **Greg Jameson**, *Best Selling Author and eCommerce entrepreneur* www.WebStoresLtd.com

"The great thing about Rob Versus The Nincompoops is that it doesn't just make you laugh; it's a blueprint for how to handle the tsunami of stupidity that being online forces you to face on a daily basis. Read it and I defy you to not get snippy with the next fool who pops up in your inbox." ~ **Jody Raynsford**, *Founder of Hello Genius and author of "How To Start A Cult"*

"Complete, non-stop hilarity (and very useful information). Sarcasm is most definitely Rob's superpower. If you read only one of Rob's books, this should be the one. But you'd be a nincompoop to make that mistake. Read them all." ~ **Steve Sipress**, *Founder of The WOW! Strategy™* www.TheWOWStrategy.com

"I gotta start with the song at the beginning...very catchy. This book does not disappoint. Humor, sarcasm, more humor and even more sarcasm. Ironically, all of it kinda fits into a lot of my everyday thoughts with interactions with people. I am pretty sure, Rob is not related to me. However, I will claim him as a pseudo nephew from here on out. Rob has to be the most unfriended/unfollowed individual I know." – **John "JP" Clark**

Table of Contents

INTRODUCTION 7

CHAPTER 1 - BEING SOCIAL, OR NOT! 9
- THERE CAN BE ONLY ONE 10
- NOT THE UPDATE HE WAS EXPECTING 13
- DISCOVERY CALLS 14
- THE JUICE ISN'T WORTH THE SQUEEZE 15

CHAPTER 2 - MEET THE STAFFORDS 19
- THE ANSWER IS YES 20
- OUR RECORDS SAY YOUR NAME IS 22
- A POLITE AND NOT SO POLITE SCAMMER 25

CHAPTER 3 - USMAN, ALEX & ISAIAH 29
- USMAN THE MIRACLE MAN 30
- JUST ALEX 31
- DREAM CLIENTS YOU SAY? 33

CHAPTER 4 - LINKEDIN LOSERS 35
- GOALS 36
- I'M THE KING OF FRANCE 37
- WHO DIS? 38
- NOT A RIGHT FIT 39
- MISTAKES WERE MADE 41
- THE SCRAPE, PITCH AND DISAPPEAR METHOD 43
- NOT A GOOD CANDIDATE 44
- LINKEDIN'S JUNIOR DETECTIVE 46
- HE WASN'T INTERESTED 47

CHAPTER 5 - NOTHING BUT SCAMMERS 49
- ABDUL & MR. KELLEY FAILED 50
- SCAMMER SCHOOL 50
- THAT'S NOT HIS NAME 54
- I SUFFER FROM SARCASM 57
- NOT TODAY 60
- IMPOSSIBLE YOU SAY? 61
- I WANT ALL OF IT 63
- SALSA AND CHIPS 65
- SOME PEOPLE ARE JUST LOUSY AT GAMES 69
- NOT A REAL SERIOUS MATTER 72
- OH YES VERY ACCURATE, NOT! 76

CHAPTER 6 - ANNOYING EMAILS 79
- It's All About The Timing 80
- Just Spam 82
- Bump and Run 84
- Can't Stop, Won't Stop 85
- Responding To Shit Emails 87
- Another Stupid Email 88
- Just Make It Stop 89

CHAPTER 7 - GRANDPA? 93
- Not My Grandson 94
- It's The Hormones 96

CHAPTER 8 - ONE MILLION DOLLARS 99
- Nope He Couldn't Handle It 100
- Non-Negotiable 104
- Revolving Lines 106

CHAPTER 9 - EVEN IN DEATH THE CALLS KEEP COMING 107
- It's Meena Again 108
- Still Dead Apparently 109

CHAPTER 10 - TIME WASTING FOOLS 111
- And My Answer Is? 112
- Oh Yes Send Me Another Audio Message 113
- Virtual Bupkis 116
- What's The Question? 118
- Common Sense Doesn't Work Here 120

CHAPTER 11 - PRICE OBJECTIONS 123
- And He Made It Into This Book 124
- Still Not A Right Fit 127

CHAPTER 12 - A JOB LIKE MINE 129
- Apparently I Have No Idea What I'm Talking About 130

ABOUT THE AUTHOR 133

RESOURCES 134

Introduction

Wowzers…what started out as an idea to share my sarcastic conversations dealing with scammers has grown into a series of books that you would think would exceed most people's amusement level. Nope.

Hey, this is book 8 in the series. And readers keep asking me for more.

So here we go. But first…

The goal of the series is to bring more laughter into the world. The biggest takeaway from the whole series is that it teaches readers how to live their lives on their own terms while learning how to not take shit from morons, the entitled, fraudsters, whackadoos, unicorns, yahoos and nincompoops.

Now get ready for some sarcasm.
Some laughter.
Maybe even some crying.
Turn the page now and let's get you started.

Enjoy.

Rob

Rob Anspach
Anspach Media
www.AnspachMedia.com

"Addicted to Rob"
Parody inspired by the original song
"Addicted to Love" by Robert Palmer:
[Verse 1]
You might as well face it, you're addicted to Rob
Might as well face it, you're addicted to Rob
Your friends, they tell you it's not right
But you just can't resist, stay up all night
He's got that charm, he's got that style
You can't help but stare and stay awhile
[Chorus]
You're addicted to Rob, addicted to Rob
Might as well face it, you're addicted to Rob
You're addicted to Rob, addicted to Rob
Might as well face it, you're addicted to Rob
[Verse 2]
He's got the moves, he's got the groove
You can't escape those eyes that soothe
You're under his spell, can't break free
Addicted to Rob, it's plain to see
[Chorus]
You're addicted to Rob, addicted to Rob
Might as well face it, you're addicted to Rob
You're addicted to Rob, addicted to Rob
Might as well face it, you're addicted to Rob
[Bridge]
He's the one you think of day and night
Can't resist his charm, it feels so right
But deep inside, you know it's not enough
Addicted to Rob, it's getting tough
[Chorus]
You're addicted to Rob, addicted to Rob
Might as well face it, you're addicted to Rob
You're addicted to Rob, addicted to Rob
Might as well face it, you're addicted to Rob
[Outro]
Might as well face it, you're addicted to Rob
Might as well face it, you're addicted to Rob

Chapter 1

Being Social, Or Not!

"Winning friends and influencing people...nope, not me!"

There Can Be Only One

Hey Rob I unfriended you.
{message appears in my Facebook messenger}

Me: Okay and?

Them: Don't you care?

Me: Not really.

Them: That's a jerky reply.

Me: Is it though?

Them: Yes it is.

Me: If you say so. But honestly I don't even know who you are. Not sure why we were friends. And, this is the only conversation we've ever had.

Them: What do you mean you don't know me?

Me: I'm sure in your mind the concept of people not knowing you doesn't exist, so glad we aren't relying on your mind.

Them: WTF man…what is your problem?

Me: Besides this nonsensical conversation I'm currently having with some delirious fool who sent me a message saying he unfriended me I have no problem.

Them: That doesn't make sense.

Me: Which part?

Them: All of it.

Me: I would agree. What kind of moron reaches out to someone saying they unfriended them, when they could have just unfriended them and never told them?

Them: It's courtesy.

Me: Since when?

Them: Since always.

Me: And how many people do you send unfriending messages to on a monthly basis?

Them: 1 or 2 at most.

Me: And do they reply?

Them: Not like you have.

Me: Thank goodness for that.

Them: Why is that?

Me: There Can Be Only One!

Them: Huh?

Me: All my friends know that phrase is from the movie "Highlander".

Them: Never saw it.

Me: Yeah, we can't be friends.

Them: You're a jerk.

{I try to respond but my message doesn't go through…apparently my new un-friend blocked me}

Note: If you've never seen the movie "Highlander" starring Christopher Lambert and Sean Connery, with the soundtrack performed by Queen, you definitely need to make it a priority to watch it. Don't watch the sequels or the TV show…just watch the first movie. Once you do that, then you and I can be friends. Yup, it's that easy.

Not The Update He Was Expecting

Hey,
I hope you are doing well.
Did you check my last message?
Kindly let me know if there is any update for me.
I look forward to your reply.

Thanks,
Mario.

{message appears in my email inbox}

Me: Hey Mario,
I'm doing well.
I haven't had a chance to check your last message.
Yes there are several updates…
I wrecked the race kart again,
The Princess has been captured,
The Mansion is filled with ghosts,
I ran out of Power Flowers,
Yoshi stopped by, he says Hello,
and everyone in the Mushroom Kingdom misses you.

See ya soon, your brother
Luigi

{pfft…5 mins later receive "We are removing you from our list"}

Discovery Calls

Do you have time for a quick discovery call this/next week?

That's the question every new connection on Facebook and LinkedIn is sending out lately.

Me: What are we discovering?
An element?
Is it the 5th Element?
Oh man say it's the Fifth Element…
Big Bada Boom.

And I never hear back from any of them.

Note: Discovery calls are the biggest waste of time… ever! Why do I need get a phone call so you can discover more about me? Why can't you just look at my social media profiles and figure it out? I shouldn't have to waste my valuable time helping you determine if I'm a right fit for your service. Stop being lazy.

The Juice Isn't Worth The Squeeze

"That's a ridiculous amount and I've always been upset with how much money she spent with you."

I received that message from a client's son after my client passed away.

So to lose a long time client (over 8 years) then to receive that message stings a bit.

I was more than fair to my client.

In fact, the last four years I refrained from increasing my rate to help my client stay afloat.

She was my lowest paying client. But she was also my friend.

Every month my client would say how much she appreciated my services and how grateful she was that I kept my prices low for her. She knew I could have charged her more. Way more.

Yet here I was reading an email from my client's son telling me I ripped off his mom.

I told him due to his attitude that we would be ceasing any and all work. I canceled the invoice that was sent 10 days prior to his mother dying, which was now overdue, and that I was willing to give them time but that was before his rant.

He blasted back, *"you're a piece of work"*.

Yeah maybe I am.

But his mom was my client.

He was not.

And seriously even if the amount was 10x more it still wouldn't be worth it to put up with this nincompoop.

Then of course like the ninny he is, he tried to be threatening with, *"maybe you've never had anyone stand up to your bullshit but I'm not the one you want to try. If you continue down this line of discourse I'll be referring you to my lawyer."*

Apparently he doesn't know me very well, or the books that I write. As the whole "Rob Versus" series deals with people like him.

So I replied with, "I'll be waiting for your lawyer to contact me. In the meantime we'll go ahead and send you the files for your websites - so that you can have them hosted elsewhere. I tried to be fair, and you turned it into a battle."

A few minutes go by and I receive, *"I didn't do anything. You've got some nerve."*

I got many nerves and he got on all of them.

So why do I share this exchange?

I share it because death happens. And those that take over the responsibility left by the deceased usually aren't prepared to deal with things. And as a contractor (vendor, consultant, service provider) you have to decide if the new management is worthy of your services. Some will indicate right away they are not a right fit. Others may give you time to mesh with their managing style. And others, well you have to decide if the juice is worth the squeeze.

Chapter 2

Meet The Staffords

"The parts of James and Annie will be played by me, of course!"

The Answer Is YES

Phone rings…Caller ID displays "Hawaii"

Me: Hello

Voice message plays: This is Health Insurance Advisors, press 1 to speak to an agent.
{so I did}

Agent: Hi, this is Mario, am I speaking to Jim Stafford?

Me: {I'm not Jim, but I answer…} Of course, who else would I be?

Mario: I see you pressed 1 to learn more about our Health Insurance rates, will you be applying for yourself or for your family?

Me: Yes.

Mario: Yes?

Me: I said Yes.

Mario: I realize you said Yes, but why?

Me: Yes is my answer.

Mario: It doesn't make sense?

Me: Yes, yes it does.

Mario: The question was, "will you be applying for yourself or for your family?"

Me: And again my answer is YES

Mario: I asked you an "either or" question not a "yes or no" question.

Me: You asked me a question which I replied YES

Mario: Okay will you be applying for yourself?

Me: Yes

Mario: See that's the answer.

Me: But I'll also be applying for my family.

Mario: You can't do both.

Me: Yes, I think I can.

Mario: No, I don't think you will.

{pfft and he hung up}

Note: If they ask for the wrong person right away, most likely the caller is a scammer and nincompoop.

Our Records Say Your Name Is

My mobile rings - caller ID says " Scam Likely"
{pfft I answer it anyway}

Recorded message plays "Hi This is Linda Davis from Debt Free America, press 1 if you'd like to eliminate your debt."

{so I press 1}

Operator: Hello

Me: Hello

Operator: My name in Meena and I'm with Rate Reduction Corporation, may I get your first name?

Me: It's Jim {the scammers call me all the time asking if I'm Jim - so if I know it's a scammer I just say I'm Jim}

Meena: You sure?

Me: Why, is there a problem?

Meena: Our records say your name is James.

Me: Yes, that's correct.

Meena: But you said Jim.

Me: Jim is a nickname for James

Meena: Is your last name Stafford?

Me: What's it say on your records?

Meena: It says Stafford

Me: Then that's who I am.

Meena: You sure?

Me: You've already asked, and I answered.

Meena: I don't believe you.

Me: Well I don't believe your name is Meena.

Meena: My name is really Meena.

Me: Well my records say that's not your name.

Meena: I guess we are both liars then.

Me: You most definitely, me not so much.

{slight pause}

Meena: My boss says your real name is Rob.

Me: Your boss is a scammer.

Boss: F-You {says in a deep gnarly voice}

Me: Meena you sound different, have you been possessed?

Boss: F-You A-Hole, I will find you.

Me: Pfft…now, now Meena, don't say anything you'll regret.

Boss: We know where you live.

Me: Cool, can you bring some Pizza and some cold brewskis?

Boss: {goes into full meltdown mode and curses at me in some foreign language}

Me: Let it all out man, can't keep that stuff bottled up.

{pfft, he hung up on me}

Note: These calls are nothing more than an attempt at getting your financial information. They will never save you money, or reduce the rate you're currently paying for your debt.

A Polite and Not So Polite Scammer

My mobile rings… Caller ID displays local number {it's a scam, but I answer anyway}

Me: Hello

Caller: {speaks with a foreign accent} Hi, my name is Kevin and I can help you with a personal loan up to $30,000.

Me: Okay, cool.

Kevin: So are you in need of funds?

Me: Sure, why not?

Kevin: Okay, can I get your name?

Me: You called me, so you should have asked when I answered.

Kevin: Oh, is this Annie Stafford?

Me: That's right?

Kevin: Is Annie your full name?

Me: Annie is short for Anakin.

Kevin: Can you spell that?

Me: T-H-A-T

Kevin: What? No, spell Anakin.
{apparently scammers don't have time to watch Star Wars movies}

Me: What other questions do you have, besides me spelling my name?

Kevin: And you live at {gives an address that is not mine}?

Me: That's right.

Kevin: That's great, I would like to transfer you to my supervisor for further processing.

Me: Okay great, put him on.
{placed on hold for 5 minutes}

Me: You still there?

Kevin: Yes Sir, my supervisor is hurrying as fast as he can.
{on hold for 2 more minutes}

Supervisor: Hi Sir, sorry to keep you waiting. Was my team member polite during his tenure with you?

Me: Yes as polite as any scammer could be.

Supervisor: You mother f-er. You a-hole. You wasted our time again.

Me: Stop calling me then.

Supervisor: We know where you live.

Me: Oh yes…come find me.

{pfft, he hung up}

Note: You'd think after all these years, and numerous books, that at least one person would take me up on my offer to visit…but they never do.

Chapter 3

Usman, Alex & Isaiah

"They promised me the world, they failed miserably."

Usman The Miracle Man

Rob,
Our team of Digital and Shopify experts is ready to schedule a call to learn more about some of the everyday pain points you might experience in achieving your desired sales.

Let's jump on a quick call to discuss this Rob. I promise I'll make it worth your while.

Talk soon,
Usman

{message appears in my email spam inbox}

Me: Usman,
So glad you emailed me. Yes, I've been concerned about the pain points for some time. I thought about scheduling with my doctor, but if your quick call can help alleviate the pain in my neck, back and knees then I'd be glad to schedule. Although right now I can't jump due to the pain, but I can hobble to the phone and after our session maybe I'll have the ability to jump again. Oh, yes I'm looking forward to this call. Your promise is like a miracle to my ears. And I'm sure when I'm healed of the pain, I'll achieve my desired sales.
-Rob

{that was 10 days ago, I don't think Usman is ever emailing me back}

Just Alex

Phone rings…Caller ID displays "Scam Likely"
{I answer anyway}

Me: Hello

Automated message says "This is Lisa from Spectrum, press 1 if you'd like to learn about our fantastic cable and streaming services, press 2 to be removed from our calling list"

{can you guess which one I pressed}

Alex: Hello this is Alex from Spectrum {says in a deep foreign accent}

Me: Sup Lex

Alex: The name is Alex not Lex

Me: Okay Alex Not Lex

Alex: What?

Me: So how can I help you Alex Not Lex

Alex: It's just Alex Not Lex.

Me: That's what I said…Alex Not Lex.

Alex: No, No, No - Just Alex

Me: Just Alex?

Alex: Yes, can we continue?

Me: Sure Just Alex.

Alex: Sir, can you give me your zip code so I can determine if we service your area?

Me: Service my area with what?

Alex: Cable and internet streaming.

Me: Oh, okay… {I give a zip code 25 miles away}

{I can hear Alex banging on a keyboard, not sure if he's typing or just making noise}

Alex: Sir, we don't service that area.

Me: Okay, then why did you call me? Seems like a lot of time wasted calling people to sell them on a service that you can't even provide.

{wait for it…}

Alex: You Sir are the one who wasted my time, you A-hole.

{and then he hung up}

Dream Clients You Say?

Hey Rob,
Your publication "Optimize This: How Two Carpet Cleaners Consistently Beat Web Designers On The Search Engines" contains great insights. How was your research process like?

My names Isaiah, and I can get you on sales calls with your *dream* clients. I promise you a sales call with 3-5 qualified prospects, and I won't charge you a dime.
The catch - I need a video testimonial (showing how I benefited you, etc.) in return. That's it.

Would you be open to a super quick call this or next week?

{Message lands in my email inbox}

Me:
Yo Isaiah,
Not sure where you are pulling your information from but that publication was like 40 books ago. As to my research process… well it doesn't rely on 9 year old information to try to win over recipients of your email.

You say you can promise me sales calls with dream clients. Well I already have actual dream clients that I can call anytime. That's what happens when you produce all the books I do…clients come to me. Pretty cool, huh? Yeah, you should try it.

As to that super quick call... I charge $1500 to listen to you (for up to 30 minutes) tell me all about how you can help me. Will you be paying with PayPal, CashApp or Venmo?

{20 minutes later}

Isaiah:
You are being removed from our list.

{I try to respond, but my email was kicked back}

Note: It's always nice to be removed from lists I never asked to be on. And, if I upset the very people who put me on the lists to the point they have to send me a message saying they are removing me well that's a bonus.

Chapter 4

LinkedIn Losers

"They don't want to be friends, they just want to sell you stuff."

Goals

Hi Rob,
How are you?
It was great connecting with you.
I wanted to reach out to get a sense of what your goals are for the next year. Is there anything on which we might be able to collaborate?

{message appears from a non-connection in my LinkedIn inbox}

Me: It was great connecting with me? As in past tense? We don't seem to be connected currently. As to my goals…I seek world domination of course. As to collaboration well I do need someone to keep my team caffeinated while we attempt world domination. Vanilla iced coffees work best. If you do that, you're in.

{pfft, he never replied}

Note: Spammers love LinkedIn! LinkedIn users however despise the constant barrage of garbage delivered to their inboxes from spammers, scammers and people wanting to get a sense of our goals.

I'm The King Of France

Hi Rob, from reading your profile I see that you are a podcaster, is that correct? Would you be willing to connect to grow each of our podcasting connections?

{message from a wannabe connection on Linkedin}

Me: Actually I'm the King of France, I just don't put that on my profile.

{no reply…but it seems his offer to connect was rescinded or he blocked me}

Note: Here's what my LinkedIn profile says…
Rob Anspach
40x Book Author / Publisher, Script Writer, Speaker, Personality Disruptor, Fractional CMO, SEO & Marketing Consultant, Host of the E-Heroes Podcast & Disney Fan

So yes, I'm a podcaster and have been since 2010 when I launched my first podcast "Passions to Profits". Then in 2017 cowrote the podcasting book "Power Guesting" and in 2018 created "E-Heroes" which now has over 250 episodes.

Who Dis?

Some health insurance agent called me using... "asdasdas asdasd" as their caller ID.

I answered - clearly they knew who I was because they said "Rob" and I replied "Nope".

They hung up and sent me a message on LinkedIn wondering why I said NOPE when they called.

So I replied "who dis".

Note: Well that's one less nincompoop that will be bothering me. So there's that.

Not A Right Fit

Email received...

Hello Rob, I saw you on LinkedIn and because we're both in real estate, I wanted to share a solution to a common pain point that I imagine you're also dealing with around creating more content for your brand. I recorded this short video for you on how we help real estate peers in our industry create more content from their existing podcast, hope you find it as helpful as they did!

Recording for Rob @ Anspach Media
Ruben

{Me responding back to Ruben...}

Ruben,
Nowhere on my LinkedIn profile does it say I'm in the real estate industry. And if you really want to solve my pain point and I would imagine everyone else's I would suggest you actually look at the profiles of the people you are sending emails and videos to.
Oh and no I did not find your video helpful.
-Rob

{After 5 days I receive...}

Rob,
If you were not interested in my email you could have simply ignored it. Responding back with your negative

tone has me wondering if you are actually a good fit for our program.
Ruben

{And I had to respond…}

Ruben,
I think I've already established that you messed up. I'm not your target audience. And seriously if you're going to email me about solving my pain point…if the pain point is caused by you…then your best recourse is to remove me from your list. See problem solved.
Rob

{Not more than 3 minutes go by and I receive…}

Rob,
Piss off.
Ruben.

{and I was blocked from sending a reply}

Note: Blasting your message to people that are not your target audience then getting angry with them when they respond with answers you don't like just makes you the king of the nincompoops.

Mistakes Were Made

Hi Rob,

I'm reaching out because I work with Founder, Chief Marketing Architect, Author, Speaker, Trust Creators of 7-9 figure E-com brands, and I did some research on your company.

I saw you guys making a few mistakes with your ad tracking and attribution that are potentially costing you between 6 to 7 figures/year in lost sales.

I'd like 15 minutes to meet because all of our clients chop their CPA in half and double or triple their ROAS within 90 days without changing anything about your ad strategy after fixing these mistakes.

I made this short video to share an overview, and my calendar is below.

<u>Click here to Watch the Video Overview</u>

<u>My Calendar - Pick a time at your convenience</u>

Cheers,
Josh

P.S.
If you think my email is irrelevant, please reply with "S" and we'll politely never email you again.

Me:
So you saw us making a few mistakes did ya?
Well your first mistake was emailing me.

Your second mistake was doing research on my company. Why would you do that? I didn't ask for you to do that.

Your third mistake was asking for 15 minutes of my time so you could tell me all the mistakes I'm making.

Your fourth mistake was sending me a video that I'll never watch.

Your fifth mistake was including your calendar that I'll never schedule.

And your final mistake was thinking I would reply "S" to your irrelevant email.

Now go away.

Note: Never point out someone's mistakes unless they ask or are paying you to do so.

The Scrape, Pitch and Disappear Method

Subject Line: Found You Through LinkedIn

Hi Rob,

I'm reaching out because you would be an ideal client for us at Design Supply. We offer companies with Product Design, UX, Marketing Graphics, and Web Development. Please let me know if it sounds interesting I'll set up a quick discovery call. Looking forward to it!
-Shea

Found me through LinkedIn...
that's code for she scraped my email address to pitch her service.

Anyhoos...
my reply back to her was...

Shea,
Ideal client you say? Hmm.
A quick discovery call?
Okay well, I charge $1500 for discovery calls and I'll listen to you pitch for up to 30 minutes. I'll send over a PayPal link so you can secure your spot with me. Once paid I will reach out with a few dates and times.
-Rob

Never heard back.

Not A Good Candidate

Hey Rob, I stumbled upon your Linkedin profile again and thought given the connections we have in common that you might be open to connect directly if we're not already?
-David V

{Message appears in my email inbox after the person scraped my email address off of LinkedIn}

Me: David V, Stumbled you say? Hmm, were you drunk, on drugs or experiencing some Neuro instability in your body's ability to walk straight? And it seems you're also experiencing some cognitive issues with memory as you don't know if we are connections.
-Rob

{25 minutes pass}

David V: Rob, You seem hostile and not what I perceive to be a good candidate for connection. Please disregard my email and have a good day.
-David V.

Me: David V, Had you actually taken the time to learn about me before scraping my email you would have discovered I probably wasn't a good connection and could have saved both of us from this conversation.
-Rob

{10 minutes go by}

David V: Rob, What is wrong with you? Stop replying. Normal people don't do this. I'm blocking you.
-David V

{I tried to respond, but my email was blocked}

Note: Hah, normal people don't write books about their adventures dealing with nincompoops either. So I have that going for me.

LinkedIn's Junior Detective

Hi Rob! I noticed we share some common connections, but our paths haven't cross yet. It would be great to have you in my network! ~ Cheers, RJ

{message appears under the invitation to connect on LinkedIn}

Me: You noticed that? So you're trying to impress me with your Junior Detective skills in hopes I accept your connection.

RJ: I sent a LinkedIn connection invite thinking you would make a nice connection. That is all.

Me: And yet you notice things like our paths haven't crossed.

RJ: It's an expression. Not to be taken literally.

Me: Well if you don't wish your comment not to be taken literally, then literally don't comment.

RJ: I simply wanted to be a connection, not have a debate on what is literal and what isn't.

Me: Now about your detective powers…is someone helping you hone your skills? I ask because it would seem you still need help.
{and I got blocked}

He Wasn't Interested

Hi Rob,
I'm looking to connect with other business owners in the area. I run a commercial roofing business here in PA, We have a really unique liquid applied system to restore your roof instead of having a costly replacement!
Have A Blessed Day! Double H Commercial Roofing
(message appears in my LinkedIn from someone who wishes to be a connection)

Me: (responding as I always do when I accept them as a connection)
Hey Henry,
I recorded a quick 15 second video
…don't worry I'm not pitching anything.
(I so dislike those people too)
Just wanted to introduce myself and wish you well.
https://youtu.be/DbyFPUAIsxs

FYI: the transcript to my 15 second video is...
"Hi, this is Rob Anspach and I want to say thanks for the connection. I appreciate you and look forward to having an awesome conversation with you.
Have a great day."

Henry: Not interested.

Me: Not interested in what? I'm not selling anything.

Henry: That's great.

Me: What's great?

{and Henry unfriended and blocked me}

Note: Sadly I never got to tell Henry I have a brand new roof and that his unique liquid applied system wouldn't be a benefit to me…but maybe he knew that, or he doesn't like my non-pitch method of actually building connections on LinkedIn. Oh Henry, we could have been besties, but you never gave it a chance.

Chapter 5

Nothing But Scammers

"And the world is safer because I waste their time."

Abdul & Mr. Kelley Failed Scammer School

HELLO DEAR,

I HOPE YOU ARE DOING WELL TODAY? I MISPLACED YOUR EMAIL CONTACT AND TELEPHONE NUMBER THAT WAS THE REASON I COULD NOT COMMUNICATE YOU FOR A LONG TIME.

I AM ABDUL ABUBAKAR RABIU, THE BUSINESS MAGNATE AND INVESTOR. I CONTACTED YOU YEARS BACK FOR AN INVESTMENT OF $150,000,000.00 USD (ONE HUNDRED AND FIFTY MILLION UNITED STATES DOLLARS) IN YOUR COUNTRY BUT LACK OF TRUST WE COULD NOT COMPLETE IT .

I HAVE RELOCATED THE INVESTMENT TO JAPAN WITH THE ASSISTANCE OF ANOTHER PERSONALITY .

HOWEVER, I DID NOT FORGET YOUR PREVIOUS EFFORTS. I KEPT A SUM OF $3,000,000.00 (THREE MILLION UNITED STATES DOLLARS) WITH DIAMOND BANK UNDER YOUR NAME. AND I WOULD LIKE YOU TO CONTACT MR. KELLEY NICKOLAS THE EXECUTIVE DIRECTOR, TREASURY & INTERNATIONAL BANKING AT

DIAMOND BANK PLC, VIA HIS PRIVATE EMAIL ADDRESS HERE SO HE CAN PROCESS THE RELEASE OF THE $3,000,000.00 ATM CARD.

I WANT YOU TO MAKE USE OF THE $3,000,000.00 (THREE MILLION UNITED STATES DOLLARS) FOR YOURSELF WHEN YOU RECEIVE IT.

I TOLD MR. KELLEY NICKOLAS OF DIAMOND BANK, THAT YOU WILL CONTACT HIM AND I KNOW HE MUST BE EXPECTING TO READ FROM YOU BY NOW.

SINCERELY,
ABDUL ABUBAKAR RABIU.
{message appears in my email inbox}

Me:
Hey Abdul,
I'm very disappointed that you lost my email and telephone number for that I suffered great emotional damage and lots of sleepless nights. So to compensate me for your lack of record keeping I will be demanding more than the $3,000,000.00 presently being offered. The new amount in demand is now $7,500,000.00. However, Mr. Kelley Nickolas may not be involved in this transaction due to deceptive practices now learned of him. Also since you wrote your entire email to me in capital letters which is a form of screaming and considered very offensive, I am insisting this transaction be expedited in 48 hours or less.
Sincerely,
Rob

Abdul:
HELLO ROB,
YOUR DEMAND FOR ADDITIONAL SUMS IS DENIED. ACCEPT THE ORIGINAL AMOUNT OR NOTHING.

Mr. Kelley:
Hello Rob,
Please explain these deceptive practices I'm accused of.

Me: {to - Abdul and Mr. Kelley}
Fellas,
It would seem that you are not being forthright with me and delaying the transfer of monies. Abdul you are still screaming at me and Mr. Kelley the charges against you are despicable and downright filthy. The fee I demand is now $10,000,000.00 and will continue to go up with every passing email exchange we have.

Abdul:
HELLO ROB,
PLEASE SUPPLY US WITH YOUR INFORMATION SUCH AS PHOTO ID, BANKING NUMBERS, ADDRESS AND PHONE NUMBER

Me:
Dude,
Stop screaming at me…the fee is now $12,500,000.00 and you can send the amount via CashApp or PayPal you have my email.
Hurry time is ticking.

Mr. Kelley:
Hello Rob,
I assure you whatever you have heard is false and that I have not committed deceptive practices.

Me: {to - Abdul and Mr. Kelley}
I don't care...the fee is now $15,000,000,00

Abdul:
NO SIR, THAT AMOUNT IS NOT CORRECT.

Me: {to - Abdul and Mr. Kelley}
I'm not playing anymore...the fee is now $30,000,000.00

Abdul:
SIR, WE CAN NOT EXCEED THE INITIAL AMOUNT, ACCEPT FIRST AMOUNT OR NOTHING.

Me: {to - Abdul and Mr. Kelley}
My fee is now $90,000,000.00 - one more comment from you and I will demand all of the $150,000,000.00

{3 days go by, I try to send another email to both Abdul and Mr. Kelley and my email was kicked back}

Note: There is no money. Never was. It's a phishing scam. All that these nefarious people want is your identity and banking or credit card information. So don't fall victim to their emails.

That's Not His Name

Home phone rings…caller ID displays a local number. {So I answer…}

Automated message plays: This is a call from your electric utility, press 1 to lower your rate and speak to an agent.

{I pressed 2 to see what will happen}

Agent: I see you pressed 1 to lower your rate

Me: I actually pressed 2, does that mean I get an even lower rate?

Agent: Sir, what is the name of your supplier?

Me: Do you mean my electric supplier or my drug supplier?

Agent: Your electric supplier who is it?

Me: Let me give you the name of my drug supplier because yours is definitely messing you up and you've apparently forgotten that you are my electric supplier.

Agent: I don't need your drug supplier's name. And we are not your electric supplier.

Me: Then why are you calling me?

Agent: To give you a lower rate with your electric usage.

Me: But your message says this call is from my electric utility so is that you are not?

Agent: Sir, we represent your electric supplier.

Me: And yet you had to ask me who they were, doesn't seem logical to me.

Agent: We know who they are, we ask to make sure they match our records.

Me: Well how can they match your records when you haven't even asked me my name.

Agent: We know who you are as well.

Me: Reaaaaalllly?

Agent: Yes.

Me: Who?

Agent: Sir, you are wasting my time.

Me: Yes, most likely, but then again…if I give you my drug suppliers name then at least it would be a productive call.

Agent: F-you.

Me: No that's not his name…not even close.

Agent: F-off.

Me: And your second guess is wrong, one more strike and you're out.

Agent: A-Hole
{pfft he hung up before I could tell him he's out}

Note: When these babbling ninnies call and don't even ask your name, it's a scam. Just go ahead and waste their time, but never give them any information that they could use to scam you.

I Suffer From Sarcasm

Hi is this Robert?
{question asked after picking up the phone displaying a local number - I was expecting a call from a contractor}

Me: Yup

Caller: Hi I'm James from the Medical Insurance Service.

Me: Okay and?

James: Our new medical insurance covers all types of injuries, ailments and afflictions that you might be experiencing.

Me: Okay

James: Can I ask if you suffer from an affliction?

Me: I was diagnosed with Sarcasm about 30 plus years ago, can your service help with that?

James: Yes, Sir… that is in fact just one of many afflictions our medical insurance covers.

Me: When I get stressed…throatpunchitis takes over and it can be very irritating to those around me.

James: Yes we can help with that too.

Me: Wonderful.

James: Can I have your credit card to sign you up and get you started?

Me: You haven't even told me a price or asked any other information from me.

James: Don't need to ask your information, we already have it. And the credit card is just so we can verify everything.

Me: Nah.

James: Sir, you are afflicted with some serious conditions, don't you wish to remedy those?

Me: Nope.

James: Sir, all you need to do is just tell me the last 4 digits of your card and we can get you started.

Me: Not happening.

James: Sir, you can trust us.

Me: Well then, if I can trust you… okay here's the numbers. N-O-P-E!

James: Sir, you are not taking this seriously.

Me: You're right I'm not. But then you're dumber than a bag of wet hammers to think Sarcasm and Throat-Punch-itis are actual medical afflictions.

{wait for it…}

James: You a-hole.
{and he hung up}

Note: When you get these types of calls, make up some weird medical condition and if they say they can help with that, it's a scam. Oh and sarcasm is not an affliction…it's my superpower.

Not Today

I rarely plug my phone into my car infotainment console…but the battery was almost dead and I figured hey the phone needs to charge. Not more than 2 minutes after plugging the phone in…the dash lights up indicating an incoming call.

The caller Id displays…"Scam Likely".
My wife looks at me and says, "don't accept".
{I press the accept button anyway}

Me: Hello

Caller: Hi Sir, this is Sam with American Solar. Have you heard about the benefits of lowering your electric dependency?

Me: Hi Sam…I haven't, tell me more.

My wife: Ah hell no…not today.
{she presses the reject call button and hangs up the call}

Me: Hey, that could have been a good story.

My wife: They'll call back, they always do.

Note: Yup, she's right…they just keep on calling.

Impossible You Say?

Mobile rings…Caller ID displays "1234"
{oh yeah, it's a scam…pfft, I answer it anyway}

Me: {not even going to say Hello - just cutting to the chase} How's this scam work?

Caller: Hi Sir…did you say your name is Sam Work?

Me: If that's what you heard, then yes, that's my name.

Caller: Hi Sam…we are with your bank and want to offer you a lower interest rate on your credit cards.

Me: My bank you say…okay.

Caller: Sir we have several people with your name on file so in order to verify your identity could you share the last 4 digits of your social security number?

Me: Well you called me so you should have that information on file. Toss out some numbers and I'll tell you if it's mine.

Caller: Sir, that's not how it works, you need to provide the information.

Me: No I don't.

Caller: Yes Sir you do.

Me: It's 1234

Caller: That's impossible.

Me: Impossible in that you don't believe me or impossible as it's the same number as your Caller ID number?

Caller: That number doesn't match and I'm wondering if Sam Work is your true name.

Me: I said at the beginning of this call "how does this scam work" and you asked if my name was Sam Work.

Caller: So instead of saying NO, you went on to waste my time.

Me: Yup.

Caller: You're an A-hole

Me: So does that mean I won't be getting a lower interest rate?

Caller: What do you think?

{and the caller hung up}

Note: If the caller ID doesn't match the company they say they represent…it's a scam.

I Want All Of It

Mobile rings…Caller ID displays "Scam Likely"
{pfft I answer it anyway}

Me: Hello

Automated message plays "This is the Financial Hardship Loan Center - you qualify for a loan up to $36k - press 1 to speak to an agent"

{so I did}

Another message plays, "Your call is being transferred with zero wait times."

{20 seconds later}

The same message plays, "Your call is being transferred with zero wait times."

Agent: Hello how may I assist you?

Me: How much money are you going to send me?

Agent: Sir, how much do you need?

Me: All of it.

Agent: And what will you do with the money?

Me: It depends on how much you are going to give me.

Agent: Sir can I get your name?

Me: I think you know who I am.

Agent: Is it Rob Anspach?

Me: What do you think?

Agent: {phone sounds muffled but I could hear} Dammit guys why did you give me this guy on my first day?

Me: Bwahahahaha

{he hung up}

Note: It's always fun getting the "trainee" on their first day. I feel so honored.

Salsa and Chips

Phone rings…Caller ID displays "Phila Daily New"

Me: Hello

Automated message plays "This is Jake from Discover Card Services, press 1 to get a lower rate on your credit card payments."

{I press 1}

Rep: Hello

Me: Hi

Rep: I'm Nadia here to help you lower your interest rate.

Me: Oh, what happened to Jake?

Nadia: Jake who?

Me: The automated message said This is Jake from Discover Card Services.

Nadia: Oh yes, he said that.

Me: Is he the same Jake that works for State Farm?

Nadia: I dunno Sir, but our records show you have about $5,000 in credit card debt.

Me: Wow, your records say that.

Nadia: Can you tell me which card has the highest balance?

Me: Huh? Your records say how much I owe yet don't tell you how much on which card?

Nadia: Can you read off your credit card expiration date?

Me: No, it doesn't have any dates or numbers on it…just a chip.

Nadia: A chip?

Me: Yes a chip.

Nadia: A chip?

{the call center is getting very noisy, hard to hear what she's saying}

Me: Can you tell everyone to shut the heck up so I can hear you?

Nadia: {says louder}
Chips?

Me: Yes all we need is some salsa and we can have a party.

Nadia: What are you talking about?

Me: Salsa and chips...doesn't that sound great.

Nadia: What would sound great is you giving me your credit card numbers.

Me: And what will do with my credit card numbers? Buy some salsa and chips?

Nadia: Stop saying salsa and chips. It doesn't make sense.

Me: It makes perfect sense if you like salsa and chips.

Nadia: There is no salsa and chips.

Me: Then you can't have my credit card numbers.

Nadia: You wasted my time.

Me: Oh, your time...
let me tell ya about your time...

(1) You call me from Philadelphia Daily News
(2) I find out that Jake from State Farm is now working for Discover
(3) There's no salsa and chips
and
(4) You seem to have this obsession with my credit card.

So, I think it's you that is wasting my time.

{wait for it...}

Nadia: F-You
{then she starts cursing at me in some foreign language}

Me: I want some Salsa and Chips.

{pfft she hung up}

Note: In most cases, the caller has no idea who you are, or what credit cards you have, or what your balance is, they are calling in hopes you will volunteer that information so they can scam you.

Some People Are Just Lousy At Games

My mobile rings…
{I didn't even bother looking at the caller ID}

Me: Hello

Rep: Sir I'm calling about your Wisa card?

Me: My what now?

Rep: Your Wisa card.

Me: Hmm, I don't have a Wisa card.

Rep: Do you have a Mastercard or Discower card?

Me: Oh you mean Visa?

Rep: That's what I said.

Me: No you said Wisa.

Rep: Sir, are you playing with me?

Me: Well, I dunno, is this a game?

Rep: Sir, I'm not interested in games, I'm here to help you.

Me: Help me with what?

Rep: I can help you reduce the amount owed on your cards.

Me: Really, any card, how so?

Rep: Yes, any card. How much do you owe?

Me: Not sure, haven't really added it all up.

Rep: Is it more than $3,000?

Me: Possibly.

Rep: Which card is that on?

Me: Hmm, I'd have to check.

Rep: Can you tell me the number of the card?

Me: {rattles off 8 numbers}

Rep: Sir, that is only 8 numbers, I need 7 or 8 more.

Me: No this card only has 8 numbers.

Rep: Sir, all credit cards have 15-16 numbers.

Me: Credit cards? Oh okay, I gave you my library card. You said you could help reduce the amount owed on cards. Well, I have lots of unreturned books that have racked up huge fees.

Rep: You are playing a game with me.

Me: Yes, and you played along so well, even though you said you weren't interested.

Rep: You A-hole.

Me: Well I won that game, ready for another?

{wait for it…}

Rep: F-You!

{and he hung up}

Note: Never ever give out your credit card number to random callers. You have no idea who they are or what they will do with your credit card information.

Not A Real Serious Matter

Phone rings…Caller ID displays "Scam Likely" {But I answer…hey if I didn't you wouldn't be entertained, so there.}

Me: Hello

{Automated message plays saying it's from Amazon and my account is being charged $1470 for an iPhone delivery and that I need to press 1 to speak to a representative. So I did.}

Rep: Hello, I see you pressed 1 {he says in a deep accented voice}

Me: Hmm, maybe, not sure what number I pressed, but anyway…what's this about?

Rep: We are tracking fraudulent activity on your account and see an iPhone worth $1470 was ordered and being shipped to Baltimore, was that you?

Me: Why would someone pay that much for an iPhone?

Rep: So that wasn't you that ordered it?

Me: Well let me check my account. Hang on.

Rep: Fraudulent activity doesn't show up on your account, that's why we are calling you.

Me: So if it doesn't show up on my account then how do you know who to call?

Rep: We have special software that tracks all activity.

Me: Oh, okay.

Rep: Sir, do you want to dispute the order?

Me: Nah.

Rep: So you did order it then?

Me: I didn't say that.

Rep: Can you give me your account number so can we verify your identity and stop the shipment?

Me: You called me, you should have all the information in front of you.

Rep: Sir we need your account information.

Me: No thank you.

Rep: Sir you will be charged $1470.

Me: Doubtful.

Rep: Sir, your account will be shut down for fraudulent activity and you will be required to pay the amount to restore the account.

Me: Okay

Rep: Sir we can take care of this right now.

Me: Nah, I'm good.

Rep: Sir how can I convince to take this matter serious?

Me: I'm glad you asked…I actually have a list just for this occasion. Go grab a pen and paper and write this down…it's important that you remember these. Okay, you ready? #1 - You have to call me by my first name, which isn't Sir. Do you even know what my first name is?

Rep: Ahh…err

Me: Now don't interrupt me…just keep writing. Onto to #2 - You need to text me a picture of yourself standing outside of your call center.

Rep: Huh? What?

Me: Dude…I said don't interrupt me - okay #3 I need a copy of your birth certificate. And #4 I need a note from your mother saying you are allowed to call foreigners to try to scam them. Okay you got all that?

Rep: No I'm not getting you a note from my mother.

Me: That's the dealbreaker…that's what convinces me that you take this matter seriously.

Rep: Wait...this isn't a scam why did you say that?

Me: Well let me see the note from your mom saying otherwise.

{Wait for it...}

Rep: Stop wasting people's time you f-ing a-hole.

Me: Does your mom know you talk like that?

Rep: {the guy loses it and stops speaking English and yells at me in some foreign language}

Me: I know, the struggle is real...how is any scammer supposed to get ahead in life if I keep wasting their time?

Rep: {I'm pretty sure he's cursing at me now}

Me: You know you could just admit defeat and hang up.

{The Rep is now joined by at least three other people who all start yelling into the phone}

Me: YES...mission accomplished. Hey, how many points do I get for wasting all your time?

{and in unison they all said...}

Reps: F-You
{and then hung up}

Oh Yes Very Accurate, Not!

Call forwards to my iPad...displays local number

Me: Hello

Caller: {Heavy accented man starts his script} Hi, I'm with your TV service and we need to update your system so you get the best experience.

Me: My TV Service?

Caller: Yes Sir, we need to send a signal through to see if your TV is up to date with the latest software.

Me: Okay, send the signal if you must.

Caller: Please wait while our system sends a signal.

{I get put on hold for about a minute as the caller supposedly sends a signal}

Caller: You still with me Sir?

Me: I'm here.

Caller: Well our test reveals your TV is not programmed with the latest software so we will need to program it for you.

Me: You don't say.

Caller: Yes Sir, our tests are very accurate.

Me: I'd say amazing…considering that the number you called me on is not associated with my TV service at all.

Caller: Sir, can you tell me what number your TV service is under and I'll look it up?

Me: Nope.

Caller: Well we can access your TV.

Me: Doubtful.

Caller: Sir do you want me to shut your service off?

Me: Sure, go ahead.

Caller: Done, your service is now shut off.

Me: And yet my TV is still on and I'm watching a show right now.

Caller: It may take a few minutes to activate.

Me: Well that's nice…but it's still on and I'm still watching a program.

Caller: I said it could take a few minutes.

Me: While we are waiting tell me how this scam works.

Caller: Sir what?

Me: You heard me…tell me how this scam works.

Caller: {starts cursing at me in some foreign language}

{then I hear someone tell him to just hang up - and that's what he did}

Note: Your TV service should have a name, that name is what should be used when calling you. Keep in mind a good majority of TV watchers are now streaming their programs from their internet provider and not their TV service. So if that's you, and you get a call from your TV service it's most likely a scam.

Chapter 6

Annoying Emails

"Don't delete them! Taunt them!"

It's All About The Timing

Hi,
Not sure if you've been really busy or you've decided to hold off for now, but I wanted to see if you might have any feedback on my last email? Waiting for your response.
Niki

{and below Niki's email to me was another equally annoying email}

Hi Rob,
Just wanted to bump my email to the top of your inbox. Let me know either way on below. Thanks.
Chris

{Both Niki and Chris attached their previous 2 (ignored by me) emails hoping their newest email would prompt me to take notice. Oh I took notice…at how lame it was and to showcase them to the world on what not to do.}

And I replied with this:
You are in direct violation of the CAN-SPAM Act and subject to the penalties of $46,517 per violation. And since you have emailed me three times in such a manner the violation penalty is now $139,551. But since I'm a nice guy I will reduce the penalty to $9551 if paid in the next 24 hours. Otherwise the full amount will be acted on and additional legal fees will be added.

{within 10 minutes I received a reply from both}

Niki: My apologies, we are removing you from our list.

{At least Niki was courteous and apologized…whether she actually follows through and removes me is anyone's guess. Chris on the other hand took a different approach…}

Chris: F-You, it's not my money and you will never find us anyway, but good luck.

Me: Here's your IP address { IP number} and physical address { gave address }.

Chris: F-You, don't care. We will continue to email you.

Me: Okay, you leave me with no other choice…sending the police to that location in a few minutes.

{unbeknownst to me, as I was just bluffing, a team of federal agents was about to raid the call center}

Chris: My apologies, I didn't think you were serious. Your team of police is here and I will comply with their commands. Again please forgive me.

Note: I still don't know if I'm being removed from future lists…but I do have incredible timing so there's that.

Just Spam

"Hey Rob, did you get my email?"
{message appears in my Facebook Messenger from some guy named George}

Me: I get lots of emails can you be more specific?

George: The one I sent you.

Me: I get on average 250 emails a day of which 90% are spam.

George: Mine wasn't spam.

Me: I bet it was.

George: No, it had an **attachment** and I made sure to BCC everyone on my list so it went directly to them.

Me: Yup, sounds like spam to me.

George: The email showcased a cool opportunity I know you would be great at.

Me: Again, spam.

George: It's not spam.

Me: If I look in my spam folder and find your email, so help me…

George: Forget it, you seem closed minded.

Me: Yes, yes, that's exactly what I am.

{pfft, he blocked me}

{and his email was in my junk folder and yes was most definitely spam}

Note: If you have to message me to tell me to look at your email…yeah, it's spam.

Bump and Run

I hope you're well Rob,
I'm just bumping my last email up your inbox and I'm out of here! Let me know if we can talk, thanks!
-Patricia

{message appeared in my email inbox}

Me:
Patricia,
You hope I'm well?
If you keep bumping stuff up my inbox it will not be well at all.
My inbox does not like that.
Seriously who taught you how to "bump and run?"
Ugh, my inbox is in so much pain now.

Rob

{27 minutes later…receive from Patricia}

WTF, we are removing you from our list, good day!

Note: Apparently some guru is teaching people to "bump" their emails as I've gotten about 50 after this exchange. It's idiotic and unnecessary. Stop doing it.

Can't Stop, Won't Stop

Dear Customer,
I trust this email finds you in good health. I'm reaching out to share an exciting prospect that involves featuring a guest post on your website.
-Rajo

Me: I charge $3500 for guest posts (blog articles) on my website. I'll send an invoice and once paid you can submit your article.

{25 minutes later}

Rajo: I am removing you from my list.

Me: I charge $5000 to be removed from your list that I never requested to be part of in the first place.

Rajo: Stop replying. I cannot afford to pay your fees.

Me: I charge $7500 to stop replying. Double when you can't afford to pay.

Rajo: No, just stop replying. If you do not like what I offer just delete and do not respond.

Me: I charge $10000 to delete your email and not respond.

Rajo: Just stop.

Me: Of course, as soon as you pay my invoice.

Rajo: F-off!

{I tried to reply but my email was rejected, guess he won't be spamming me through that email again}

Note: Unless you absolutely know the person who wants to put a blog article on your website, then your answer should be a resounding NO! Getting a random message from some nincompoop about an exciting project should immediately send up red flags.

Responding To Shit Emails

I've received about 3 dozen emails from people in the last week all starting off with "I hope you're well". And every single email followed that phrase with some product or service they want me to buy. Ugh.

(1) Do they know something I don't about my health?
(2) Why does that phrase even need to be there?
(3) It's like 1 second of caring followed by 359 seconds of not giving a shit.
(4) The people writing these emails need to learn marketing.
(5) The people writing these emails need to be kicked in the jimmies a few times to be reminded to learn marketing.
(6) Why not just start the email with... "Hey I see you opened this email, that's a clear sign you're not dead. Congrats on that by the way. Now let me share with you something that'll make your toes tingle and give new meaning to living your life to the fullest..." then tell me more about your product or service.
(7) Or they could go the honest route with the email by starting out with... "Hey I just got kicked in the jimmies for sending out shit emails...I know you probably don't care, but let me tell you I can barely walk. It hurts when I cough. And as much as I want to share with you my pain, I need to sell you some stuff, so here we go..."
(8) Stop asking "I hope you're well" because some sarcastic writer will go on a rant, make a list, and share it out wasting everyone's time who reads it.

Another Stupid Email

Hi Rob,
Your details were shared with me by our research team. I'm a media researcher with a 'pay on results' PR firm. I find it fascinating how Anspach Media helps doctors, lawyers, and professionals dominate their niche using digital media, publishing, and sales conversion techniques. As an expert in social media, podcasting, entrepreneurial coaching, publishing, copywriting, pay per click, ghostwriting, and search engine optimization, I thought you might be interested in a media request we have that aligns with industry trends closely relevant to your business. Can I share it with you? Also, we have other media requests that could be an even better fit for you. What do you think?
Best,
Thank you,
Larry
P.S. Just a quick reminder that you won't have any upfront costs to deal with. Also, I'm adding a team member to this email so we can keep everything in check. When you get back to us, please be sure to hit "respond all." Thanks!
Sent from my Verizon, Samsung Galaxy smartphone

Me:
Oh yes, the classic "your details were shared with me".
And then you decided to spam my inbox.
Now go ahead and remove my name from your list.

Just Make It Stop

I order a product online…to which I get…

Email #1 - A welcome email thanking me for becoming part of their family

Email #2 {2 minutes after Email #1} - Telling me what a great selection I made and my order is now being sent to "George" for processing.

Email #3 {5 minutes after Email #2} - My product is being handed off to "Jenny" for inspection.

Email #4 {4 minutes after Email #3} - Apparently now "Javiar" is packing my item and getting it ready to ship.

Email #5 {6 minutes after Email #4} - Telling me my item has shipped. Also offers me a 10% discount if I order again.

Email #6 {1 minute after Email #5} - A receipt for my purchase.

{an hour goes by}

Email #7 - Hey we see you haven't taken advantage of the coupon yet, here's a special code to get 15% off.

{I'm contemplating waterboarding myself}

{another hour goes by}

Email #8 - Not even sure what it says as I'm scrambling to find the Unsubscribe button.

Email #9 {10 seconds after I click unsubscribe} Sorry to see you go, it may take 2-3 days before your email is scrubbed from our lists, you may in that time experience a few more emails from us.

{wondering what hell I got myself into}

Email #10 {an hour later} Please take our customer satisfaction survey it helps us improve.
Email #11 {20 minutes after Email #10} I see you didn't take our survey yet, could you do that now.

{takes survey in hopes to end the madness}

Email #12 {a minute after completing survey} A welcome email thanking me for becoming part of the family.

{picks up the phone to call the lunatics at this business to which I get an automated message stating "due to heavy call volume hold times are exceeding 4 hours, to better assist you go to our website chat service and start an inquiry}

{goes to website chat service - message pops up stating "you have reached us after hours or all representatives are busy. Enter your name and text number and we will contact you when a representative is available}

{I know it's a trap…but I feel I've already committed to this and need to see where it goes.}

Text #1 - You are number 113 in the queue.
{30 seconds later}

Text #2 - You are number 110 in the queue.
{45 seconds later}
Text #3 - You are number 98 in the queue.
{then in rapid succession get 4 texts in a row}
Text #4 - You are number 77 in the queue.
Text #5 - You are number 63 in the queue.
Text #6 - You are number 52 in the queue.
Text #7 - You are number 27 in the queue.
{then nothing for 5 minutes}
Text #8 - You are next in line for a phone call - is (XXX-XXX-XXXX) your phone number press YES to confirm.

{I press YES}

{5 minutes later receive}

Text #9 - Sorry. We tried to call you.

{UGH!}

Note: And if you're wondering why companies are failing. It's because they stopped offering real customer care.

Chapter 7

Grandpa?

"Not today! And tomorrow doesn't look promising either."

Not My Grandson

Well it finally happened…I got the Grandpa call.

My mobile rings…Caller ID displays a Chicago number.

Me: Hello

Caller: Hi Grandpa {says with a slight accent}

Me: What?

Caller: Hi Grandpa

Me: Who is this?

Caller: It's your Grandson.

Me: Doubt it.

Caller: Sorry to wake you Grandpa, I need help.

Me: You need something alright.

Caller: I'm in Chicago and I need money.

Me: That sucks for you.

Caller: Grandpa I need help.

Me: Yeah, you said that.

Caller: Can you help?

Me: No

Caller: But I'm your Grandson.

Me: Well...
(1) you sound too old to be my grandson
(2) my grandson doesn't have an accent
(3) my grandson is not a scammer and
(4) he would identify himself using his name.

Caller: F-You Grandpa

Me: Yup definitely a scammer.

{he hung up}

Note: It's sad that these scammers resort to these tactics, sadly though, people fall for it and they lose lots of money.

It's The Hormones

My mobile rings...caller ID displays "Scam Likely"

{I answer it anyway}

Me: Hello

Caller: {guy with a deep raspy voice} Hi Grandpa.

Me: {me playing along} What ya need boy?

Caller: Hi Grandpa

Me: So which of my grandsons are you?

Caller: I'm your oldest grandson.

Me: Must be the hormones or something.

Caller: What did you say grandpa?

Me: The hormones in the milk must be messing with you.

Caller: Grandpa I need help.

Me: You need to lay off the hormones.

Caller: Grandpa I need money.

Me: What you need son is to stop scamming people. My oldest grandson is only 10 and doesn't sound like he smokes 2 packs a day.

Caller: F-You Grandpa

Me: Don't make me come kick your ass boy.

Caller: F-You

{and he hung up}

Note: If you have friends, relatives or neighbors over the age of 50 help them understand that these types of calls are scams. Make sure they ask questions. Lots of questions. If they say they are a grandson, granddaughter or any relative for that matter - ask for their name and a call back number. Always verify. And never ever give financial information over the phone.

Chapter 8

One Million Dollars

"Pfft, I thought it was fair."

Nope He Couldn't Handle It

Phone rings…Caller ID displays "United States" { I answer it anyway}

Me: Hello

Caller: Hi this is Sam from All-Star Mortgage is this Ryan?

Me: {I'm not Ryan, but he doesn't know that} Yo, what can I do for you?

Sam: Do you own the property at {XXXX Street} in Albuquerque, New Mexico?

Me: Maybe. What's this about?

Sam: Would you be willing to sell it?

Me: Sure… for about a million dollars.

Sam: {laughs a bit} That really seems high for the property.

Me: What were you expecting me to say?

Sam: Not a million dollars, at best it's worth $200k

Me: {I laugh this time} So now you're insulting me by undercutting the value of the home by 80%

Sam: Sir, I don't mean to insult you, but that's the going price of the home.

Me: I want a million dollars…and I'm not going to budge.

Sam: Sir, Mr. Ryan, Sir…you only bought the property 12 months ago.

Me: Well I did a lot of improvements.

Sam: Can you tell me what improvements you made to the property?

Me: No.

Sam: Sir, if you want the maximum price, I need to be able to understand how you justify asking for a million dollars.

Me: {at this point I was getting bored with the convo} Dude, if you can't get a million dollars stop wasting my time.

Sam: Your house isn't worth that much.

Me: And this is why you can't sell the house. You have no confidence.

Sam: I do so have confidence I can sell anything.

Me: Great, sell the house for a million dollars.

Sam: Except that.

Me: Goodbye Sam

Sam: No wait…let me try.

Me: Nah. You're so weak…I don't think you could handle it.

Sam: I can, give me a shot.

Me: If you sell it for a million dollars, I'll pay you $100k, I'll keep $500k and I'll give the owner $400k which is double what he bought it for last year.

Sam: Wait what?

Me: It's a win/win/win everybody makes some money.

Sam: Go back to the part where you give the owner $400k

Me: Yeah that's what I said.

Sam: So you're not the owner?

Me: Nope.

Sam: Who are you then?

Me: I suppose some random stranger, a number you misdialed, but fortunately you got me, some people are really greedy and I reckon would just pay you the 6% commission, I'm offering $40k more to make it worth your time.

{wait for it…}

Sam: You're a real f-ing jokester…you wasted my time you a-hole. If I ever find you I'll…

Me: {I cut him off before he could finish} I take it you don't want to sell the property then. Man, we all could have made some money.

Sam: F-You

{and he hung up}

Note: Not sure how all these nincompoops get my phone number, but I sure do have fun with them.

Non-Negotiable

My mobile rings…yup, you guessed it…
"Scam Likely"
{but I answer it…hey it's what I do}

Me: Hello

Caller: This is John I'm calling about your property, we would like to buy it.

Me: Okay, 1 million dollars.

John: Is that price negotiable?

Me: Nope.

John: Is there something special about the house that makes it worth that much.

Me: Yup.

John: Can you tell me what that is?

Me: Well John, you know those mystery toys that you buy for kids, you really don't know what the toy is until you actually open it, yeah it's like my house.

John: So you're saying it's a mystery.

Me: Now you're catching on. Yup, a big ole million dollar mystery.

John: Yeah I don't think so.

Me: Oh it'll be fun.

John: No I think you're a jerk for wasting my time.

Me: I think you need to stop eating paint chips and get a sense of humor.

{wait for it...}

John: F-YOU!
{and he hung up}

Note: On the plus side he never called me back. And he must've told Sam as he never called back either.

Revolving Lines

Via text:
Hey, it's Sandy from Commercial Partners, with our new revolving line of credit you can get up to $1M, starting at 4.25% - Are you interested?

Me responding back:
Hey, it's Rob with my new revolving line of throat punches - first one is FREE - are you interested?

Apparently not, as she never replied.

Note: You'd think offering something for free and people would be all over it. Well, their loss.

Chapter 9

Even In Death The Calls Keep Coming

"The Grim Reaper Call Center is now hiring."

It's Meena Again

Phone rings...caller ID displays a Harrisburg PA #
{I answer it}

Me: Hello

Caller: Hi, I'm Meena from the Healthcare Department, I'm just calling to see how you are doing.

Me: I'm dead.

Meena: I'm sorry you are dealing with that. But don't worry we are here to help.

Me: Help with...resurrection?
Turning me into a zombie?
What?

{pfft Meena hung up}

Note: Most callers are just following a script and they rarely listen to what you say, but occasionally you'll get someone who pays attention (as in the next story).

Still Dead Apparently

Mobile rings…Caller ID displays Oklahoma number.

Me: Hello

Caller: How are you today?

Me: I'm dead.

Caller: I'm sorry Sir, I didn't catch what you said.

Me: I'm dead. I died. I'm deceased. I'm no more.

Caller: Oh okay.

{Caller hangs up}

{A minute goes by…}

My phone rings again…same number.

Me: Hello

Caller: You still dead?

Me: Yup.

{The caller hung up again}

Chapter 10

Time Wasting Fools

"Sarcasm is the only thing that works against these people."

And My Answer Is?

Mark: Hi Rob I'd love to find out about how things are going at Anspach Media. Just a quick question. I'm working with a small group of business owners to help them to generate 5 to 10 new clients within 90 days. Just wondering if you'd be interested? Cheers Mark

Me: Hey Mark, Things are going awesome here at Anspach Media despite the constant barrage of consultants sending us quick questions wondering if we'd be interested in 5 to 10 new clients over a 90 day period.

What's really annoying about it is these same consultants (who have very little experience being consultants) think generating leads is the thing that most entrepreneurs desire.

And yet, if they just took the time to look at their prospects profile and read a few of their posts they would get a better sense of who their prospects were and how to really help them.

No stupid quick questions, no lame promises of so many leads....none of that. So back to the question of "If I'd be interested?"

I think you already know my answer. It's NO!

Oh Yes Send Me Another Audio Message

Hey Rob I would love to have you on my podcast. {message drops into my Facebook inbox}

Me: Okay, send me a calendar link.

Some Ninny: {leaves a 2 minute audio message}

Me: Hey I'm not in an area where I can listen to your message - can you type it out?

Some Ninny: I don't like to type {leaves another audio message}

Me: I have no idea what your audio messages are, so if you wish me to be on your podcast just send me a scheduling link.

Some Ninny: {Sends link and leaves another audio message}

Me: Dude, I told you I'm not in an area where I can listen to your message, why do you keep leaving them?

Some Ninny: It's easier {proceeds to leave a 4th message}

{So I blocked him}

{10 minutes go by and I get an email from the guy}

Some Ninny: Hey, not sure why you blocked me, but I'd really like for you to be on my podcast. Here's my scheduling link {leaves URL}.

Me: And you couldn't type that to me in Facebook Messenger?

Some Ninny: I prefer leaving audio messages.

Me: I prefer short conversations, but here we are.

Some Ninny: Can you unblock me so we can use messenger, I dislike typing.

Me: Nope. I think this conversation is over.
{I blocked his email}

{15 minutes later…he sends me a message through LinkedIn}

{I didn't respond, just blocked him.}

{Then my phone rings…I let it go to voicemail…it's him…ugh}

Some Ninny: Yo, Rob, WTH…stop blocking me and give me a chance. I think you'd make a great podcast guest.

{Me blocking that number}

Note: I went back and played the messages from Facebook and he suggested I could share ideas on how I deal with people who waste my time. I guess he will never know.

Virtual Bupkis

"Hey Rob we are doing a virtual event and we would like you to be a speaker."
{message drops in my Messenger inbox}

Me: Why?

Virtual Nincompoop: Because we think you would be great.

Me: I would be…but I'm sick of virtual, so no.

Virtual Nincompoop: Well, you know we still have this Covid thing going around.

Me: Yep, I've had it…doesn't change how I feel though.

Virtual Nincompoop: So you don't want to do it.

Me: Give me a real stage to speak on and I might consider it.

Virtual Nincompoop: But this a global stage with attendees from every continent.

Me: Yeah, but it's virtual, so no.

Virtual Nincompoop: It's real easy though…you promote the event to your lists and you'll receive a percentage of any sale generated from the unique link we give you.

Me: Definitely not then.

Virtual Nincompoop: I don't understand…all of our speakers are working this way.

Me: I'm not.

Virtual Nincompoop: Well that's how this event works.

Me: Doesn't work for me. Count me out.

Virtual Nincompoop: You could make millions off of your time during the event.

Me: Most likely I make bupkis.

Virtual Nincompoop: What is that? Bupkis?

Me: Means nada, zip, zilch, zero, diddly squat…got it. Nope! Not happening.

Virtual Nincompoop: You could have just said No to begin with instead of being so rude.

Me: {rolling my eyes} Yeah it's my fault. I apparently didn't convey my negative desire about this event in a manner you would understand.

{wait for it…}

Virtual Nincompoop: You're an a-hole.
{and I got blocked}

What's The Question?

Can I ask you a question?
{message lands in my Facebook inbox}

Me: Was that it?

The Question Guy: Was what it?

Me: That's two now.

The Question Guy: Two what?

Me: You are up to three now.

The Question Guy: What are you talking about?

Me: Okay, that's four.

The Question Guy: : What is going on?

Me: You are now up to five.

The Question Guy: : Ah, okay…yes, hahaha…very funny.

Me: You asked 5 questions and seriously I'm tired now.

The Question Guy: Well I didn't ask you the question I needed to.

Me: Don't care anymore.

The Question Guy: But I need to ask you the question.

Me: Please don't, you already wasted too much of my time already.

The Question Guy: So you're not curious as to my question?

Me: Ugh, here we go again.

The Question Guy: You're a jerk.

Me: Oh, yes, it's my fault you wasted my time with 5 questions and you still haven't asked the right one.

The Question Guy: Do you act like this to everyone?

Me: Was that the question you needed to ask or yet another question that has nothing to do with what you needed to ask?

The Question Guy: Ugh, you're impossible.

Me: And you waste so much time trying to ask one question, next time just lead with the question you need to ask and stop wasting people's time.

{and I got blocked}

Note: Keep it simple and lead with the question you need to ask.

Common Sense Doesn't Work Here

Noticed my oil tank was at the 1/4 mark (meaning that in a short time it'll be empty). So I called the oil company.

Me: Hi this Rob Anspach (I give my address) and I need to schedule a heating oil delivery.

Call taker: I see you are on automatic delivery which is scheduled for October.

Me: Okay but I'm at the 1/4 mark and will probably run out of oil before then.

Call taker: So how much oil will you need?

Me: Well I don't know. How about the tech just fill the tank?

Call taker: If he fills the tank then you won't be needing an automatic delivery in October.

Me: How about you fill the tank now and come October you fill whatever it needs then.

Call taker: No can do, that throws off our automatic delivery schedule.

Me: How so? Your driver will still be driving through the neighborhood in October so stopping by my house won't take but a few minutes.

Call taker: Sir, that is not how automatic delivery works.

Me: Well, I don't want to run out of fuel.

Call taker: Sir I will speak to my manager and call you back.

{20 minutes go by and the call taker leaves a message on my voicemail}

"Hi Robert, I talked to my manager and he said he's OK with a driver delivering fuel for you now but you will pushed back one month for automatic deliveries. Hope that makes sense. Thank you, bye."

{Me calling back}

Me: Hi this is Rob Anspach you left a message on my voicemail telling me how the automatic delivery will work going forward. How about I just call when I need oil. Then we don't have to worry about your automatic deliveries being screwed up. I can just order when I need to.

Call taker: I guess that will work.

Me: Yes, that's what I figured too.

{pfft the call taker hung up}

Chapter 11

Price Objections

"They choose poorly."

And He Made It Into This Book

OMG Rob you raised your Kindle price of your new book already.
{message drops in my Facebook chat}

Me: Yup, you should have ordered when it was on pre-order status.

Them: I thought I had more time.

Me: Well you didn't. So now the price is $4 higher.

Them: Doesn't seem fair.

Me: It doesn't does it. Two weeks of non-stop posts and emails telling people that my new book was on preorder status and to take action I suppose was not enough time for you.

Them: No I was busy.

Me: And those that took advantage of the preorder price weren't?

Them: I don't know, but I don't want to pay $4 extra.

Me: Well I didn't want to have this conversation, yet here we are.

Them: Are you going to sell me the Kindle for a cheaper price?

Me: Nope.

Them: Why not?

Me: One, you snooze and you lose, tough break. Two, if I change the price, then all those who bought at the higher price will be mad. And three, I really don't want you reading it.

Them: Why?

Me: Why to 1, 2, 3 or all of it?

Them: Never mind, I'm not sure why I even bothered you over $4

Me: On the bright side…you made it into the next book.

Them: No, I don't want this conversation going anywhere beyond here, especially in your books.

Me: I suppose you should have thought about that before you sent me a chat.

Them: How much to keep this out of your books?

Me: So you go all cheap on me about a $4 increase over buying my book and now you're offering to pay me to keep you out of my next book…is that correct?

Them: Yeah, how much?

Me: I think I'll just keep you in the book.

Them: I just bought your book on Amazon, does that make you happy now.

Me: Awesome, and when the book comes out with your conversation, I'll let you know so you can buy that one too.

{wait for it...}

Them: You F-er.

{and I got unfriended and blocked}

Note: So much effort expended over $4, imagine how much BS he causes over more money.

Still Not A Right Fit

Hi Rob,

We would love to offer an exclusive paid article for Rob Anspach to be featured on Inquirer.

A little about us:
- Our Domain Authority 89 | DR 85
- 24 million monthly active users

Here is a link to view traffic stats & Media Kit

By publishing an evergreen article targeting the right keyword clusters and with a backlink to your website tells Google that your brand is an authoritative source of information and would rank higher in search results.

Articles are permanent and exclusive to your brand. We have a wide range of headlines we can target with keywords related to your niche.

Would you like me to send over a few article topic ideas?

Best,
Leland

P.S. If it's easier, we can set up a quick 15-min meeting to go through some of the topic ideas. Please let me know what times work best for you, or you can book through my calendar link.

Me:
Leland,
I charge $1500 for an article - how will you be paying?
Rob

{an hour later}

Rob,
Thank you for your response, at this time we don't feel like you are a right fit for our service.
Leland

Note: Leland didn't argue, he didn't haggle, he just cut to the chase and said I wasn't a right fit. That and he couldn't afford my fee.

Chapter 12

A Job Like Mine

"With great power, pfft, just show me the money!"

Apparently I Have No Idea What I'm Talking About

Hey Rob I want a job like yours.
{message drops into my Facebook Messenger}

Me: Fine give me $5 million and it's yours

Guy: I don't have $5 million dollars.

Me: Then you can't have a job like mine.

Guy: But don't you own the business?

Me: Yes, yes I do and I spent over 28 years learning how to make what I do profitable.

Guy: Wow, that's too long.

Me: It is a very long time. But if you wish to skip all the steps needed to learn how to do everything I did to become successful, then it's $5 million and you can have my job.

Guy: Again I don't have $5 million.

Me: Or the patience to earn it properly.

Guy: You always this rude?

Me: Yes. Especially to people who think wanting a job someone else does will make their life easier.

Guy: That's not what I said.

Me: Isn't it? I think that's exactly what you said. And frankly, if you're not willing to put in the time, nor the money and follow your own dreams then you will always follow the dreams of someone else.

{oh yes wait for it...}

Guy: F-You. You have no idea what you are talking about.

{and I got blocked}

Note: Most people don't see the struggles, the long days and nights, the sacrifices...all they see is how easy it looks. Yeah, it looks easy because I spent decades honing my skills to make it look that way. Sadly, most people who want to be entrepreneurs aren't willing to put in the time.

About The Author

Rob is affectionately known as "Mr. Sarcasm" to his friends - to everyone else he's a Certified Digital Marketing Strategist, a Foremost Expert On Specialized SEO, a Serial Author, Podcaster, Speaker and Authority Broadcaster who can help amplify YOU to your audience.

Rob has also produced books for many clients including lawyers, doctors, copywriters, speakers and consultants.

Rob helps companies across the globe generate new revenue and capture online business. And he hates scammers with a passion.

Rob is available to share talks and give interviews.

To learn more about Rob visit **www.AnspachMedia.com** or call Anspach Media at **(412)267-7224** today.

Resources

THE INTERVIEW SERIES FOR ENTREPRENEURS

Rob Anspach interviews talented entrepreneurs who demonstrate an eagerness to share their experiences, their knowledge and their stories to help others succeed.

Listen to the Rob Anspach's E-Heroes Podcast today.

Available on:

Apple, Google, I Heart Radio, Stitcher, Spotify, Pandora

Or

www.AnspachMedia.com

Rob Versus The Scammers

Protecting The World Against Fraud, Nuisance Calls & Downright Phony Scams.

Available on Amazon in Print & Kindle
www.RobVersus.com

Rob Versus The Morons

Overcoming Idiotic Customers With Wit, Sarcasm And A Take No Bullshit Attitude

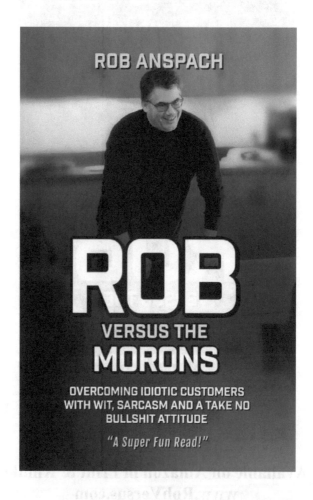

Available on Amazon in Print & Kindle
www.RobVersus.com

Rob Versus Humanity

The Last Line Of Defense In Outwitting, Outlasting and Outliving Time Wasters, Fraudsters And Fools.

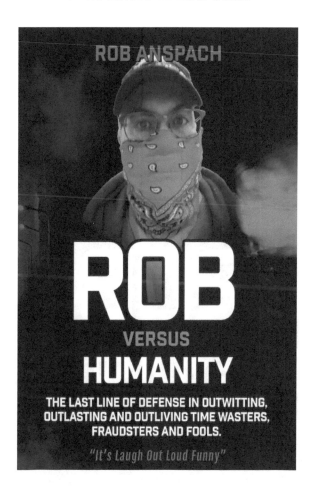

Available on Amazon in Print & Kindle
www.RobVersus.com

Rob Versus The Entitled

Defeating The Aggressive, Offended, And Easily Triggered With A Little Common Sense & A Lot Of Sarcasm.

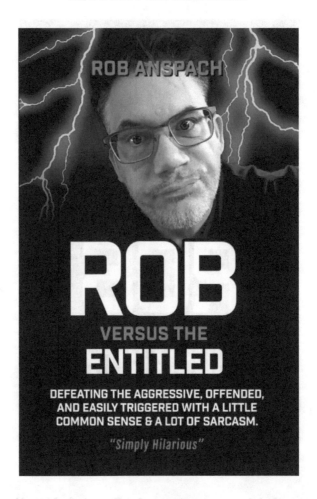

Available on Amazon in Print & Kindle
www.RobVersus.com

Rob Versus The Whackadoos

Conquering Ridiculous Attitudes and Scammy Behaviors With Lightning Fast Wit
& Shearing Sarcasm.

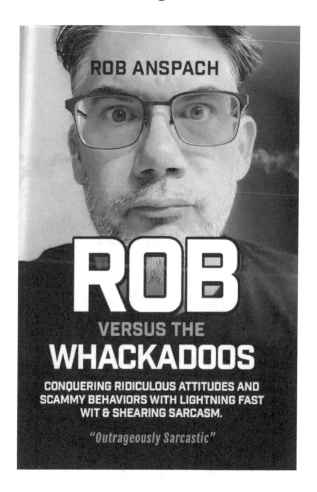

**Available on Amazon in Print & Kindle
www.RobVersus.com**

Rob Versus The Unicorns

Repelling The Mystical, Malevolent And Borderline Idiotic With Spells Of Sarcasm, Wit & Humor.

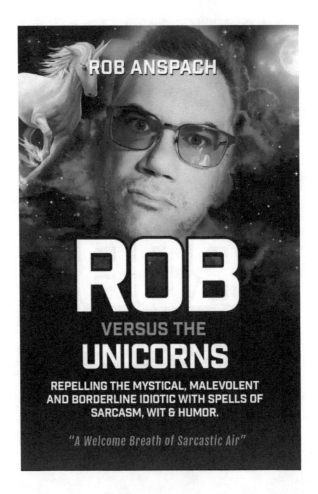

Available on Amazon in Print & Kindle
www.RobVersus.com

Rob Versus The Yahoos

Taming Bloated Egos
And Obnoxious Behaviors With Rapier
Wit & Sensational Sarcasm

Available on Amazon in Print & Kindle
www.RobVersus.com

Rob Anspach

Books Produced By
Anspach Media
That You Might Enjoy

To learn more visit https://AnspachMedia.com/books

Remember to…

Share This Book!

Share it with your friends!

Share it with your colleagues!

Share it with law enforcement!

Share it on social media.

Share it using this hashtag...

#RobVersusTheNincompoops

Made in United States
Troutdale, OR
11/10/2023

14456041R00086